◆ In Celebration of ◆

_____

A special book
for your
special day!

_____

Place & Date

_____

Name

Wishes

_____

_____

_____

_____

_____

_____

_____

_____

Picture of the day

_____

Name

Wishes

_____

_____

_____

_____

_____

_____

_____

Picture of the day

_____

Name

Wishes

_____

_____

_____

_____

_____

_____

_____

Picture of the day

Name

Wishes

Picture of the day

Name

Wishes

Picture of the day

Name

Wishes

Picture of the day

_____

Name

Wishes

_____

_____

_____

_____

_____

_____

_____

Picture of the day

Name

Wishes

Picture of the day

Name

Wishes

Picture of the day

Name

Wishes

Picture of the day

Name

Wishes

Picture of the day

Name

Wishes

Picture of the day

Name

Wishes

Picture of the day

_____
Name

Wishes

_____

_____

_____

_____

_____

_____

_____

Picture of the day

Name

Wishes

Picture of the day

_____

Name

Wishes

_____
_____
_____
_____
_____
_____
_____
_____

Picture of the day

Name

Wishes

Picture of the day

Name

Wishes

Picture of the day

_____
Name

Wishes

_____

_____

_____

_____

_____

_____

_____

Picture of the day

Name

Wishes

Picture of the day

Name

Wishes

Picture of the day

Name

Wishes

Picture of the day

Name

Wishes

Picture of the day

Name

Wishes

Picture of the day

Name

Wishes

Picture of the day

Name

Wishes

Picture of the day

Name

Wishes

Picture of the day

Name

Wishes

Picture of the day

_____

Name

Wishes

_____

_____

_____

_____

_____

_____

_____

Picture of the day

Name

Wishes

Picture of the day

Name

Wishes

Picture of the day

Name

Wishes

Picture of the day

Name

Wishes

Picture of the day

Name

Wishes

Picture of the day

Name

Wishes

Picture of the day

Name

Wishes

Picture of the day

_____

Name

Wishes

_____

_____

_____

_____

_____

_____

_____

Picture of the day

Name

Wishes

Picture of the day

Name

Wishes

Picture of the day

Name

Wishes

Picture of the day

Name

Wishes

Picture of the day

_____

Name

Wishes

_____

_____

_____

_____

_____

_____

_____

_____

Picture of the day

Name

Wishes

Picture of the day

_____

Name

Wishes

_____

_____

_____

_____

_____

_____

_____

Picture of the day

Name

Wishes

Picture of the day

Name

Wishes

Picture of the day

Name

Wishes

Picture of the day

Name

Wishes

Picture of the day

_____
Name

Wishes

_____

_____

_____

_____

_____

_____

_____

Picture of the day

Name

Wishes

Picture of the day

Name

Wishes

Picture of the day

Name

Wishes

Picture of the day

Name

Wishes

Picture of the day

Name

Wishes

Picture of the day

_____

Name

Wishes

_____

_____

_____

_____

_____

_____

_____

Picture of the day

_____

Name

Wishes

_____

_____

_____

_____

_____

_____

_____

_____

Picture of the day

Name

Wishes

Picture of the day

_____
Name

Wishes

_____

_____

_____

_____

_____

_____

_____

Picture of the day

Name

Wishes

Picture of the day

Name

Wishes

Picture of the day

Name

Wishes

Picture of the day

_____

Name

Wishes

_____
_____
_____
_____
_____
_____
_____

Picture of the day

Name

Wishes

Picture of the day

_____
Name

Wishes

_____

_____

_____

_____

_____

_____

_____

Picture of the day

Name

Wishes

Picture of the day

Name

Wishes

Picture of the day

Name

Wishes

Picture of the day

_____

Name

Wishes

_____

_____

_____

_____

_____

_____

_____

_____

Picture of the day

_____

Name

Wishes

_____

_____

_____

_____

_____

_____

_____

Picture of the day

_____

Name

Wishes

_____

_____

_____

_____

_____

_____

_____

_____

Picture of the day

Name

Wishes

Picture of the day

_____

Name

Wishes

_____

_____

_____

_____

_____

_____

_____

Picture of the day

_____

Name

Wishes

_____

_____

_____

_____

_____

_____

_____

Picture of the day

Name

Wishes

Picture of the day

Name

Wishes

Picture of the day

Name

Wishes

Picture of the day

Name

Wishes

Picture of the day

_____

Name

Wishes

_____

_____

_____

_____

_____

_____

_____

Picture of the day

Name

Wishes

Picture of the day

_____

Name

Wishes

_____

_____

_____

_____

_____

_____

_____

_____

Picture of the day

Name

Wishes

Picture of the day

Name

Wishes

Picture of the day

Name

Wishes

Picture of the day

_____

Name

Wishes

_____

_____

_____

_____

_____

_____

_____

_____

Picture of the day

Name

Wishes

Picture of the day

_____

Name

Wishes

_____

_____

_____

_____

_____

_____

_____

Picture of the day

Name

Wishes

Picture of the day

Name

Wishes

Picture of the day

Name

Wishes

Picture of the day

Made in the USA
Las Vegas, NV
23 February 2024

86119072R00103